If These Fields Could Talk

The Untold Story from Leatha Jackson
Queen of BBQ

Leatha Jackson

with Matthew Jordan

INDIGORIVER
P U B L I S H I N G

If These Fields Could Talk

The Untold Story from Leatha Jackson
Queen of BBQ

Leatha Jackson

with Matthew Jordan

If These Fields Could Talk : The Untold Story from Leatha Jackson Queen of BBQ

Editors: Adam Tillinghast, Donna Melillo, Christian Pacheco, April Miller
Cover Design: Jason Kauffmann / Firelight Interactive /
          firelightinteractive.com
Cover Photo: Jim Leben / www.jimleben.smugmug.com
Interior Design: Rick Soldin / book-comp.com

Special thanks to Charles Everhart for your contribution to this book.

Special thanks also to the Mississippi Oral History Program. This book would not have been possible without their evocative interviews of Leatha Jackson.

Indigo River Publishing
3 West Garden Street Ste. 352
Pensacola, FL 32502
www.indigoriverpublishing.com

Ordering Information:
Quantity sales: Special discounts are available on quantity purchases by corporations, associations, and others. For details, contact the publisher at the address above.
Orders by U.S. trade bookstores and wholesalers: Please contact the publisher at the address above.

Printed in the United States of America

Library of Congress Control Number: 2013955218

ISBN: 978-0-9860493-3-0

First Edition

With Indigo River Publishing, you can always expect great books, strong voices, and meaningful messages.
Most importantly, you'll always find ... words worth reading.

This book is dedicated to family, my friends, and to my late husband Columbus Jackson, whom I had the privilege to have known, loved, and lived with for over forty years. It was he who instilled in me as his wife that I can do anything I set my mind to do, just as long as I put my trust in God.

Contents

Only Two Dollars in My Purse

*J*will never forget that cold day in the winter of 1949, as I sat on a bus heading to Bogalusa, Louisiana. I had decided to leave my abusive husband Pearlye once and for all. I had also made up my mind to leave Franklin County, Mississippi. I'd had enough of the poverty and struggle and bigotry that ran so deep in those parts. It was time for me and my little daughter Myrtis to get away. I figured as long as I stayed, my life would never amount to much of anything. My little girl mattered most now. She deserved a better life, and I intended to see that she got it.

It had taken a while for me to work up the courage. I really hated to leave my husband, but I was tired of the abuse, and I was worn down by his alcoholism. I held a special place in my heart for Pearlye—after all, we had a child together—but I had to get out, and I had to do it then, while I still had the nerve. His drinking had gotten worse, and I was beginning to fear for my safety and the safety of little Myrtis. She was only four. She was precious, and it was up to me to protect her. I had to cut ties with Pearlye.

I watched innocent little Myrtis drift off to sleep in the seat beside me, and I thought about how life changes folks. Pearlye wasn't always mean-spirited. At one time, he was a caring husband and a good father to our little girl. I wondered if it was the years of not being able to find decent work, being belittled as a man because of his skin color, and the liquor that finally took its toll on him. Lord, I just didn't know. Here I was, deserting him without any warning, because I knew that he would never allow me to leave him. This was the only way out.

I had heard a lot about Bogalusa, Louisiana. I heard it was a place where a black woman could make her mark and become somebody. Bogalusa was a small town in Washington Parish, near New Orleans, where my Auntie Emma Levi lived. She ran her own restaurant, and I'd always had a deep admiration for the life she had made for herself there. I'd heard about all of the ways Bogalusa was different than Franklin County. It was just a bus ride to Louisiana, but it seemed a world away to me.

The past was heavy on my mind as the bus blew up dust on the dirt roads behind us. The sun was just coming up, and little Myrtis was asleep beside me. I held her hand and I cried as I thought about my own early years. I did have some wonderful memories of growing up in spite of what we lacked, but I wanted more for my daughter. I was twenty-five years old, and I was leaving my past behind. I had only two dollars in my purse; but I had God in my heart, my little girl by my side, and a dream for a better future.

The Mind Tends to Wander

I was born February 22, 1923, into a world that I did not choose. We were dirt poor. I was the fifth of fourteen children. We lived on a small farm in McCall's Creek, Mississippi, in a little run-down shack with only two beds.

My mother and father slept in one bed, and the girls mostly slept in the other, along with a couple of the younger boys. The older boys slept on the floor on a makeshift pallet. The children who slept in the bed slept four at the head of the bed, four at the foot of the bed. Yes, Lord, it was always crowded at our house, but we made do.

My daddy would get up early in the morning to make wood for the old pot-belly stove, milk the cow, and collect a few eggs from the chickens so we could have breakfast. When there wasn't enough milk or eggs to feed all of us, we sometimes had cat-head biscuits and syrup, which I didn't mind at all. That was my favorite as a child. Many days, though, when times were really rough and food was short, we ate nothing but "mush." Mush was made by cooking a little lard and corn meal in boiling water. Mama would throw salt in to give it some flavor, and we'd eat it for breakfast, lunch, and dinner. Keeping the hunger away for a day or a week was about all mush was good for, but there were plenty of times that we were hungry enough to be grateful for it.

Mississippi was mostly black at that time, although that was changing because so many black folks were migrating north for jobs. Later on, they called it the Great Migration. Opportunities were scarce, but some stayed behind. Most of the black folks who stayed behind were poor sharecroppers like us, doing their best to survive. We didn't have much, but Mama and Daddy always made sure we had clothes on our backs and some kind of food in our bellies.

My mother was quite a woman. I was named after her—Leatha—and I was proud to share her name. She did whatever she had to do to help us get by. She worked the fields too, and I can remember her going hunting for game, fishing, and cleaning the meat she caught.

My daddy, Tower Hillard, worked for wage hands, making fifty cents a day to farm other folks' land. He was also a preacher. Growing up, we were all grounded in the word of God, thanks to Daddy. Sometimes at night I could hear him praying, asking God to help him support his family.

School wasn't a priority with so many mouths to feed. I went to an all-black school when I was little—naturally, because of the Jim Crow laws—but I had to drop out in the third grade to help my mother take care of my other sisters and brothers. There was a lot of taking care of to be done. I enjoyed school, and I did dream of getting a diploma, but it wasn't meant to be. That's just the way it was in those days, and I accepted it. We all did what was necessary. Someone had to help keep my younger brothers and sisters out of the fire.

From the time I was eight, I was either watching out for the younger ones or working the fields. We all worked the fields on our little farm as soon as we got old enough to follow instruction. We had cotton, corn, potatoes, peas, butter beans, and okra. After we got older and stronger, we'd work other folks' fields to help make ends meet.

Some of my dreaming about a different life started in those fields. The mind tends to wander during a long day of planting seeds under a hot sun. I imagined myself becoming a successful woman someday—maybe even a businesswoman. I imagined a life with a devoted husband and children who didn't have to work and sweat in the fields or eat mush for dinner or lack for anything. I imagined being part of a community that accepted and even loved my family, and I imagined ways we could give that love back. In my daydreams, I just knew I could do whatever I set out to do. I had that spark inside me from early on, somehow, and I guess it never went out ... but it would be many long years before I'd reap what my dreams had sown.

Life Was Heavy

I was still dwelling on my past as the bus rumbled on toward Bogalusa. The early morning sun hadn't quite melted the frost on the windows, so there wasn't much to see yet. Little Myrtis was still asleep beside me. We were near the back of the bus, as we had to be in those days, and I wondered if things might be a little different for Myrtis as she got older. It sure wasn't easy to make your way as a black woman, even in a state as black as Mississippi.

My family never caught the worst of the racism growing up, but I'd heard tell of a lynching, in some other parts of the state, from time to time. The Ku Klux Klan was like a real-life ghost story in those days—you might not see them, but you knew they were around—and that was scary to think about as a black child.

Everything was segregated; and as a little girl, I was too small to do anything but accept it and abide by it.

White folks had advantages we didn't have, even the poor ones, and that's just the way it was.

I suppose it's natural to wish for what you don't have. Truth be told, even though I was loved and cared for by my parents, I dreamed of being taken in by a white family when I was growing up. There was a nice couple we used to pick cotton for when I was little. They didn't have any kids of their own. They were fond of me, and they would beg my daddy to give me to them. Lord knows, sometimes I wished he would give me to them. I remember thinking I wouldn't have cried nary a time, because if I went with them, I could have finished school and had more opportunities in life. I would have missed my family, sure enough, but I would have held that inside.

I even became best of friends with a little white girl named Mary Alice. Her family accepted me, and we played together all the time. She used to love to play with my hair and fix it different ways, and we really enjoyed each other's company. Maybe we were too young to notice that some folks might've looked at us funny when we were together. We didn't care. We stayed friends, too, even after we got older and realized that the world saw black and white a little differently than we did.

There was no getting around it, though—I was a black girl, and I was going to become a black woman who most likely had a hard road ahead.

My mother's life was what was typical in those days. She would work hours in the cotton fields. Then she would come home, cook us a meal, bathe the younger kids, and get us ready for bed. After a while, she would be so tired, Lord, she could barely keep her eyes open. She didn't have a lot of time to spend with her children that didn't involve some kind of work on her part. Life was heavy.

I knew the life I had growing up had toughened me up, though, no matter where my road took me, and toughness is a gift that'll get you out of a scrape or two. Shoot, I once grabbed a big, old wood rat with my bare hands to keep him off of our food, and I stopped his clock. I was a tough young thing. But I knew I didn't want to struggle like my Mama forever—and I knew I didn't want that struggle for Little Myrtis or any daughters I might have to come.

I looked at Little Myrtis again, still sleeping peacefully in that seat beside me. The sun had just melted the frost on the windows, and I saw green land stretching out beside her. Life hadn't gotten rough for her yet. Not yet. I said a little prayer that maybe it wouldn't have to.

No Use in Crying

I drifted off for a little shut-eye myself during that bus ride. I faded in and out, dreaming and waking up, with life and dream blending together the way they do sometimes. I drifted back to my teenage years when I spent longer and longer days in those fields—and the sun coming through that bus window took me back to a hot sun beating down in a sweltering field. I drifted back to cold winters gathered around a pot-belly stove for heat as Mama made mush for dinner. I remembered that old ache in my belly and the warm desire for something with more meat and substance and flavor. I remembered the kinship we all felt together as a big family under the same roof, cutting up and making each other laugh because there wasn't any use in crying.

When you're sharing a shack with two beds among sixteen people, finding a little space does cross your mind from time to time. I was nineteen when I married Pearlye and found a little space of my own. We'd met on the dusty dirt roads of Franklin County, and I thought he was what I wanted. But sometimes space will leave you exposed. I wasn't as safe as I was before, and it became worse with time.

You're more exposed to *everything* when there's just two of you—and when you're young. Lord, it's true. You're more exposed to racism—the open kind *and* the kind that sneaks up on you. You're more exposed on that hard road to make ends meet. You're more exposed to the fear of coming up short or flat-out empty. You're more exposed to the temptations of liquor.

The less work there was for Pearlye, the more he drank, and I was still working the fields. Little Myrtis came along, but we were even poorer than my folks had been. To call our place a shack would have been an insult to shacks. Lord, it was hard for a black family to make it in Franklin County at that time. We couldn't handle more children in our circumstances, and there wasn't any way for our circumstances to change. The only thing changing was Pearlye. The circumstances were changing *him*, and it was getting ugly. It was just a matter of time before ugly crossed over into something else.

So here I was, breaking free. It was best for everyone—
Lord knows I was easing Pearlye's burden too. I'd spent
enough time bending over in fields, living in fear, and
accepting circumstances. This was the only way to make
circumstances change.

The bus pulled to a stop, and I squinted into that
morning glare. Some folks shuffled off the bus, some
shuffled on. "Next stop, Bogalusa!" the driver shouted.

I was as nervous as I was excited. I didn't know what
the future was going to bring, but I whispered to Little
Myrtis, "We're almost there, baby."

I Needed a Haven

Reaching the Bogalusa city limits after a bumpy ride on a chilly bus, I felt some relief. As I stared out the window, I noticed people walking up and down the streets. The sun was shining bright, but I saw the winter coats of some of the women blowing against the harsh winds as they walked on the sidewalk. It appeared to me that this might be a nice place to live, but I knew only time would tell. I took little Myrtis by the hand, and we headed to the forward passenger area so that we could step off and set our feet in Bogalusa.

We had a good walk ahead of us, and we took our time. I knew my Auntie Emma would be busy at her restaurant in the afternoon, and I didn't want to bother her until she was winding down for the day. I could see lots of black-owned businesses open on the main street as we passed by. In some ways, it seemed as though we had left the racist past and entered into a kinder future. I couldn't believe what I was seeing. I couldn't believe there were so many black-owned businesses nestled together. It only added fuel to a fire already burning inside of me to someday open my own business.

I took little Myrtis into some of the stores to warm up and to see first-hand the kinds of things black folks could enjoy in better circumstances.

After we'd walked around downtown Bogalusa for a few hours, Myrtis was getting tired, and I figured Auntie Emma would be cleaning up for the day. I'd come to town with directions to her restaurant written down, and we headed that way. I had spoken to Auntie on the phone, and she knew we were coming, but I still felt uneasy about what I was asking of her.

We approached her restaurant, located in a little building right across from the paper mill. I peeked in a window and saw Auntie by herself, sweeping up inside. I stepped to the front door. I figured the door was unlocked, and there was no need to knock, but I knocked anyway. I was shaking in my shoes.

I knew Auntie was a loving and kind person, but I wasn't there for a visit. I was looking for a haven for me and my child. As I stood there, I could hear footsteps moving swiftly toward the front door, and I began to tense up. I said to myself, "Relax. It's only my Auntie, my mother's sister," but my mind was racing.

There was so much I wanted from her—maybe too much. I wanted to ask her about my mother, about what she was like before the world became so heavy for her. I was hoping she could tell me more about Mama because in some ways, as a child, I never really got a chance to know her. I also wanted to learn everything I could from Auntie. I wanted to learn about how she'd made so much of her life. I wanted to learn how a black woman could change her circumstances and make it in a world stacked against her. I needed a haven and so much more. I heard the footsteps reach the door. The knob began to turn, and I squeezed little Myrtis' hand tight.

The Lord Led Me There

*A*untie Emma opened the front door of the restaurant, and I could see her little round face, black and grayish hair, and her beautiful smile. She spoke with a soft voice, saying, "Hello, girls," and she gave me and little Myrtis big, warm hugs. After all that worry, I felt so welcomed—so accepted right away. That was my Auntie.

She led us inside, and we sat at one of the little wooden tables near the front and caught up for a while. Then I helped her finish sweeping and tidying the room. The place wasn't much to look at, but I loved everything about it. It was warm and cozy, and just being there set my mind all the more at ease.

After we were done tidying up, Auntie Emma said, "Let's get on home."

Auntie Emma lived nearby, and her house was so well kept and beautiful. Growing up in Franklin County, all I saw in the black neighborhoods were old rundown shanty houses with rusty tin roofs. In fact, you could actually stand outside and look straight through some of the houses. They were poorly built; most of them had deep crevices, broken windows, and broken-down porches and doorsteps. My Auntie's house filled me with pride. For a black woman to own a house like hers was a blessing.

When I entered the house, the first thing I noticed was the beautiful new furniture set in the living room. "Wow, Auntie," I said, "I've never seen so much nice furniture in my life!"

She said, "Child, all this was given to me by God. I take no credit for any of this. If you put Him first, all these material things shall be added. Never forget that."

"I sure won't, Auntie," I said.

"Come on. I'll show you to your room," she said. "I know y'all must be tired and hungry." She was right about that. We hadn't eaten anything since leaving Franklin County. "You'd better let your Auntie put some old Southern cooking in your belly before you pass out," she said. "Why don't y'all go wash up while I heat you up something to eat?"

As Myrtis and I bathed in Auntie's nice porcelain tub, I couldn't help but notice the smell coming from the kitchen. Whatever she was cooking smelled wonderful, and I couldn't wait to sink my teeth into it.

After a while, Auntie brought out all the food she'd prepared and set it on the kitchen table. I could see golden-brown cornbread, collard greens with neck bones, candied yams, fried chicken, and fried okra. I'd never seen so many dishes on the table at one time. We sure didn't have that much to choose from back in Franklin County—we ate whatever we could manage to put on the table.

Once Auntie set the table, we sat down to eat. And I have to say I had never tasted such food in all my life. She could sure enough cook! Right then, I wondered, if I asked her, would she teach me how to cook a meal like this?

That dinner sure did me a world of good, and even little Myrtis cleaned her plate and asked for more. After eating, I helped Auntie clear the table and wash the dishes. She made me feel so at home right off the bat. I could see why my mother was so fond of her. She was truly a remarkable woman, and I hoped she would take me under her wing. I still had a lot of growing up to do, but I realized that if there was anybody in this world who could teach me how to make my way in life, it would be my Auntie. The more I thought about it, the more I felt that God had brought me to her doorstep. The Bible says, "The steps of a good man or woman are ordered by the Lord!" I knew the Lord had led me there, and I couldn't help but to thank the Lord for his goodness.

Grab an Apron

For years I'd known some of the story, but I quickly learned just how my Auntie Emma had become so successful. She was smart enough to open her little restaurant, called *Levi*, right beside the Bogalusa paper mill. At noon, the men who worked at the mill would break for lunch, and before long, they came to love Auntie's food. She would fix quick foods like hamburgers and hot dogs, which folks would gobble right up, but she would also make a blue plate special—a meat and two vegetables—for men who wanted a full meal. Lunchtime was the big rush, but she was also famous for her cobblers, pies, and cakes, which she would sell all afternoon long. Men would take them home to share with their wives and children, and their families were always begging for more. Yes, Lord, that location by the paper mill was as sweet as her desserts, and everyone loved Auntie Emma.

On my second day in Bogalusa, she took me and little Myrtis to the restaurant with her in the morning. I saw with my own eyes that Auntie could work some magic in a kitchen. She seasoned most of her meats and vegetables with salt meat. Most folks call it fat back, and Auntie showed me the wonders it can work when it's time to season some food. She would use only fresh vegetables—greens, beans, peas, and so forth—and season them slowly until your mouth watered. People just don't season food any more, not the way my Auntie did. And her desserts were something to behold ... coconut cakes that tasted like they were made in heaven, and those great big pies and cobblers with only fresh fruits, nothing at all from a can.

I watched her work for a while that day, seasoning vegetables and kneading dough and pouring her love into her cooking, and somehow I knew I had found my own calling. "Can I help, Auntie?" I asked. I think she could tell by the way I said it that I wasn't asking as a guest—I was asking as a woman who was looking to get to work in that kitchen. "You surely may, honey. Grab an apron and get over here," she said.

Looking back, I probably made a mess of things that first day, but I followed Auntie's instructions. I'll never forget the excitement when that crowd showed up for lunch. To see all of those hardworking, hungry men enjoying food that I'd helped to prepare was a satisfaction I'd never felt before.

But it was the way Auntie prepared food that really stuck with me. It was like the good Lord was guiding her hands when she made a peach cobbler. She gently smoothed her homemade crust around the pan, sliced up fresh peaches, seasoned them just right, and laid them carefully on that crust. Then, with just as much care, she spread another crust over the top. She baked that cobbler to a golden brown; and when she pulled it out of the oven, it was the most perfect dessert some folks had ever laid eyes on or tasted.

When that first day wound down, we cleaned up and set out a slice of peach cobbler for little Myrtis, who had been well-behaved even with all of the bustle going on. I'm telling you, she had a mouth full of that cobbler when she said, "Can we stay here, Mama?"

Auntie and I laughed together. Everything about that day just felt right. This was where I belonged—where we belonged—at least for a while. I never got much schooling in my day, but I knew I had a new teacher in my Auntie Emma.

Easy Grace and Courage

As the days passed in Bogalusa, I continued to be blessed by all that Auntie taught me, but my thoughts would often drift to my family and folks back home. It occurred to me that everything I'd learned from my mama and daddy growing up was a gift as well. There is education to be had everywhere in this life if you open yourself up to it.

My folks helped to guide me along my path before I even understood there was a path to be on. You see, when I was coming up, even though we lacked what a lot of folks had, we found a way to make some occasions special. Christmastime was most special of all, and my mama taught me to make cakes and pies for the holiday. Looking back, I believe that's where my love for cooking first began, standing by my mama's side when I was a young girl and making something that we couldn't enjoy every day of the year.

Lord knows, though, the lessons Mama and Daddy taught me went way beyond cooking. They carried me through my childhood, and I knew they'd carry me through in Bogalusa, too.

"Be consistent in what you do and what you say," Daddy always said.

"You have to be able to trust in order to learn," my Mama would say. I thought about these words when I put my trust in Auntie, and I was never more rewarded by following a piece of advice.

Mama and Daddy would both say, "Show me your company, and I'll show you who you are." That's a wisdom that didn't sink in right away for me, I'll confess. But it's one I came to live by.

They also showed me how a loving couple looks out for one another. Daddy couldn't read, so Mama would read the Bible to him so he could prepare his sermons for Sundays. And Daddy made sure we always respected Mama. I hoped to have that kind of a bond with a husband someday.

I was learning new things every day at the Levi in Bogalusa, but I realized that my parents were my first teachers, and they were something special. Somehow they managed to serve the Lord, make time for each other, and watch out for all fourteen of us kids when they barely had two pennies to rub together. I remember talking one night to Auntie about my mama and daddy. We talked about all the burdens they handled and how they accepted them with such easy grace and courage. And I remember her saying, "Maybe running a restaurant isn't so tough after all, honey."

I Thought
I Was in Love

When you're young, you tend to be foolish at times, and I was still young. My life wasn't all cooking and praising the Lord when I was in Bogalusa. I was courted by men from time to time, and I was looking to find the right man to share my life with.

I liked one young man in particular. He was a true Louisiana charmer. He swept me off my feet and had my head spinning, and I thought I was in love. I fell for him, soon enough. It wasn't until I was carrying his child that I learned that half the women in Bogalusa had fallen for him too.

This man had no interest in being a father or a husband, and I had no interest in sharing him with the rest of the women in Bogalusa. Our fling ended as fast as it began, and I was going to be a mama again.

I prayed to God to give me guidance and wisdom, and I had Auntie's love and support. I learned so much from the experience. I learned a little more about the nature of some men, and I learned how tough I had become—taking a stand and breaking away from my ex-husband had made me stronger. The whole thing was a blessing, in many ways. I always trusted that whatever happened in my life was part of God's plan for me, and this was no different.

When my little boy was born, I named him Ive Ville. He was a sweet baby and a gift from God, indeed. His natural father would never be a part of Ive Ville's life, but that didn't mean that he would never have a daddy. I always kept the faith that the right man—the man I was really meant to spend my life with—would still come walking into mine someday.

More on His Mind than Just the Food

The paper mill always brought hungry workers into Levi to fill their bellies, but it wasn't the only business that sent a lot of folks our way. Railroad workers would come in from time to time, and they were just as worn out and just as hungry. Some of them became regular customers while they were working in the area, which was no surprise to me. Everyone loved the food at Levi.

I'd been working with Auntie for four years when Columbus Jackson came walking through our doors. He was a carpenter by trade and worked the railroads. I noticed him right away, and he seemed to notice me. He started coming back, day after day, and he always made a point of smiling and saying "hello" to me, while his eyes lingered on mine. I began to suspect he had more on his mind than just the food. Auntie saw it too. Every

time Columbus left the restaurant, she would whisper,
"That man is sweet on you, child."

That suited me just fine. I thought he was a handsome, strapping man, and he seemed to be a gentleman.
I also liked that he was a man who respected God—I
noticed he would always take a few moments to pray
before a meal.

After a few weeks, Columbus sidled up beside me
after finishing his lunch and said, "Leatha, I'd be mighty
happy if you'd let me take you out this weekend." I
nearly dropped the plate I was carrying, but I said,
"That'd be nice, Columbus," and tried my best to keep
from smiling too widely.

As soon as we starting courting, I knew there was
something different about Columbus. He was the kind of
man I always imagined I could marry and make a life with.
He was a hard-working man with big dreams, and we
were both of the same mind about a great many things.

Most people called him Brud Jackson, as in Brother
Jackson, and that was something I took to calling him
myself: Brud.

What pleased me most was that he had a natural
and kind way about him when he was around Myrtis and
Ive Ville. Columbus was a widower, and he had an older
daughter of his own, named Glentet, who was grown

by the time I met him. When Glentet was just a baby, her mama died, and Columbus—as a single, widowed railroad worker—wasn't able to raise Glentet himself. Her grandma raised her, but Columbus had always paid for her groceries and clothes and everything else she needed and had spent every weekend with her that he could. He was a caring man, and it was easy to see that he was born to be a father. He just needed a wife by his side.

Columbus was also from Mississippi. We both had rough times growing up, but his story amazed even me. When he was a little boy, his daddy wasn't around, and his mama passed away. With no place else to go, he wound up living with his aunt and uncle. They were dirt poor. And when he was just seven, he overheard them talking one night about how they couldn't afford to feed him. He heard his own uncle tell his aunt to go get an axe and to kill poor little Columbus with it ... so that there would be one less mouth to feed.

His aunt never looked out for Columbus like she should have, but he never imagined she'd go so far as to kill him. He was wrong. His aunt went to get that axe. Little Columbus was terrified, but he was a survivor. He grabbed a hammer and decided he would fight his way out. When his aunt returned with the axe, Columbus was holding and swinging that hammer. Somehow, in the commotion, he held his aunt and uncle off just long enough to bust out of the house and escape. He disappeared into the fields and never returned again.

He wandered about until he was taken in by some white folks who lived miles away. They wondered how that little boy came to be adrift, and he told them his story. They were compassionate folks, and they took a liking to little Columbus. From that time on, they raised him as one of their own.

That must have been quite something in Mississippi in those days—white folks raising a black child. I admitted to Columbus that even though I was loved and cared for by my parents, I dreamed of being taken in by a white family myself growing up.

As you might imagine, the white family that took little Columbus in had to defend him from the hatred of others who weren't so kind. Once, he was swimming in a nearby pond with some of their other children. Some white folks showed up and didn't appreciate a black child swimming in their water, so they chased Columbus, intending to do him harm and maybe even kill him. Columbus and the kids ran back home, and the white woman who looked after him stepped out of that house and stepped between Columbus and that mob with a shotgun. She told those other white folks to leave Columbus alone, or else.

The past wasn't always a pretty thing to talk about, but Columbus and I would go for walks on Saturday and Sunday afternoons, talking about the past and about what we wanted and hoped for in the future. We didn't talk much about the present, I suppose, but that present was mighty nice.

They say some folks are destined to meet, and that's what it felt like during my courtship with Columbus. We were shaped by our days coming up in Mississippi, and we were building a fast and powerful love for each other, walking hand-in-hand through the streets of Bogalusa.

It Would Mean Moving Back to Mississippi

The Lord surely does work in mysterious ways. My growing love for Columbus meant that my days in Bogalusa were winding down. Columbus did most of his work in Foxworth, Mississippi, and a life with him would mean leaving Auntie and my work at Levi. It would mean moving back to Mississippi, and I wasn't sure if I'd be taking a step backward or forward. I was sure that I loved Columbus, though, and that he'd make a fine husband, as long as he did just one thing for me.

Columbus liked to drink, like other men I'd known, and this was something I'd lost all tolerance for. It was a way of life for some, I suppose, and common among men working the railroad. I guess it was harmless enough for some folks, but I'd seen it cause plenty of harm myself. I couldn't bear the idea of spending the rest of my life with a man and his liquor.

After courting for a few months, we were out strolling one warm evening in Bogalusa, and Columbus dropped to a knee. That sweet man proposed to me, and I was mighty touched by it, but I knew I couldn't say yes right away.

"Baby," I said, "I love you, and I do want to marry you. I'll go with you anywhere the Lord leads us. But you have to make me a promise first." My eyes were filling with tears, but I had to say what I needed to say, and he had to know I meant it, "You have to promise me you'll give up drinking. I've seen too much of the devil in it. You have to promise me, Brud, and you have to keep to it. You take your time with it if you need to, but if you do that … and if you give your love to me and my children … then I'll say yes and be yours for the rest of my days."

I could tell he expected me to say something a little different, and he didn't know what to say next. It was quiet for a good minute after that. There was nothing but cicadas doing their humming and the sound of cars in the distance. I still had tears in my eyes, but Lord knows I was firm in my resolve. I looked down at him, and bless him, his eyes were wet too. He took my hand and slowly slid a ring on my finger. It wasn't some fancy thing, but it was beautiful to me. That thoughtful man had been scraping and saving up for it as best he could with his railroad wages. "Sweetheart," he said, "There ain't no need for you to cry. Shoot, I couldn't even enjoy another drink if it meant passing my days without you. You've got my word, Leatha. I don't need it, and I won't taste another drop. I'm making that promise here and now. Let the unmarried fellows have at it."

He stood up, and I wrapped my arms tight around him, and he wrapped his around me. "Okay, baby … okay then," I whispered. I still had tears in my eyes, but they were flowing for something good now, for a life filled with hope and promise, and for something I knew deep down was meant to be. And just like that, I was engaged—happily bound to become Leatha Jackson and destined to make my way back to Mississippi.

We're Going Home, Sweetheart

My return to Mississippi didn't happen right away, as everything moved a little slower in those days. Columbus was set on building us a house in Foxworth first—building it with his own hands. After we got married, I kept on working with Auntie, and Columbus would travel back and forth as his job allowed, building our home in one town and visiting me in another. We didn't talk much about the past anymore during those visits. Our eyes were set on the future.

I enjoyed my last couple of years working with Auntie, soaking up what I could about cooking and seasoning, running a restaurant, and making crowds of hungry folks happy. I learned the traditional ways to make all kinds of southern food, but my special gift—if God blessed me with one—was a knack for seasoning a meal just right. Chicken, pork ribs, beef ribs, and steaks. There wasn't any set of rules to stick to. Seasoning to my own taste—and *trusting* my own taste—was the secret above all, and that's the most important thing Auntie ever taught me.

When Columbus would visit, we would talk about starting up a restaurant in Mississippi someday, Lord willing. It was my dream, and it became a dream we shared. Whatever we'd do, we'd do it together. He'd also tell me about the home he was building for us and how it was all coming together, nail by nail. We talked about having more kids someday—and truth be told, we weren't holding back in the trying.

Myrtis and Ive Ville kept me busy when I wasn't busy cooking. Myrtis was getting to an age that she could help me look out for her little brother for a few minutes when I needed it. I would teach her a little something here and there about cooking, but she had to keep an eye on Ive Ville when Auntie and I were watching that grill. Those kids must have felt like they grew up in a kitchen, Lord knows, but there's nothing wrong with that—not when so many kids go hungry.

In a different sort of way, I grew up in that kitchen too. I became so close with Auntie during my years there that I knew it would be mighty hard saying goodbye when the time came to move on. She had provided a home, a job, and a fresh start in life. She was a great teacher and a sweet and caring woman of God. The Lord had led me to her doorstep, but now he was leading me on another path, and she understood that.

Even though we'd only be a short ride apart by road or rail, it surely broke my heart to leave her. But as God Almighty planned, Columbus put that last nail in the house he'd been building for us, and I had a husband and a home to go to.

The big day came, and Columbus came with it. As he helped us pack up, I thought about that bus ride to Bogalusa seven years earlier. Everything felt so uncertain then, but there was nothing uncertain about the trip we were about to take. Columbus was going to show us our finished home. We were going to be a family, once and for all.

There were plenty of tears at the bus station on that Sunday afternoon in 1955. Auntie hugged us all goodbye, squeezing the children tight. Before we got on board, she gave me one last hug and said, "Leatha, put God first, put this beautiful family a close second, and put your cooking third, and you will be blessed in every way. I love you, child."

"I love you too, Auntie," I said.

As the bus pulled out of the station, the children and I waved to her from the window. Little Myrtis kept on waving, bless her heart, until we couldn't see Auntie anymore and the station was small in the distance. Soon, Bogalusa was small in the distance too, and then it was gone.

Columbus, who had put in so many long days of toil and sweat to make a dream happen, leaned his seat back, took my hand, and said real softly, "We're going home, sweetheart."

If I Ever . . .

Our new life in Foxworth was what we hoped for in most ways—we had each other, we had a roof over our heads, and we had food on the table—but we were still poor folks working for low wages, just scraping by, and dreaming of a little something more. Columbus had his railroad job, and I worked for a little while as a short order cook at the Sands Motel making hamburgers, fried chicken, fried fish, and quick stuff like that before moving on to work for a white man named Nick Lewis at Nick's BBQ.

Nick was a good fellow, and I enjoyed working for him. We didn't own a car, so Nick would pick me up in the morning and drive me home at the end of my shift. I did it all at Nick's BBQ—dinner cook, dish washer, bottle washer—you name it. Auntie had made some barbeque at Levi, for folks who wanted it, but it wasn't really her specialty because she had to make it on the stove since she didn't have a grill to work with. Nick had a big outdoor grill, and I learned right away, that's the best way to make real barbeque. Shoot, if you cooked like that inside, you'd smoke yourself out. You've got to cook that barbeque on an outdoor grill. Folks can smell it from a mile away, but it smells so good, they won't ever mind.

Nick had his own set way of doing things, like any barbeque cook should—his own way of making the sauce, and his own style of preparing and cooking the meat. I was respectful of that, and I stuck to doing things the way Nick wanted them done. But I had my own ideas about how I might do things a little differently, if I ever had a place of my own.

Columbus and I still talked and prayed about opening up a restaurant someday, but we had to get over a hump or two to make it happen, and there was never enough money to try. We had land by the house where we kept a big garden with butterbeans and so forth, and we thought it might make a nice spot for a restaurant one day. But we were just imagining what might be possible down the road.

We were blessed that Myrtis and Ive Ville had it a little better than we did as small children, and that was enough to be grateful for. I had worked the fields as a child, and little Columbus had nearly been killed just because food was so scarce. This was a better life. The Lord had provided for us; and if there was more that we were meant to have, we knew the Lord would provide it in His own good time.

You Didn't Give
Us Our Sugar!

Nothing has brought me more joy in life than being a mother. After a couple of years, we were well settled in at our home in Foxworth, and God must have decided that the time was right to bring some new souls into the world. He blessed us with Bonnie in 1958 and Carolyn just a year later. They added so much to our home and our hearts.

I was also reminded that God will test your strength and resolve from time to time, because one year after that, Columbus Junior was stillborn. The Lord decided to keep that precious little soul in heaven, as He sometimes does.

Four years later, little Larry came along. Larry was born with a mental disability, but a child has never been born with a sweeter way about him or a bigger heart.

Two years after Larry, little Barbara was born, and she was also mentally disabled. Just like her brother, she had such a good heart. The Lord must've decided that we were a family who could watch over kids who needed it most, and I believe He chose well. We loved those precious children.

Columbus was my rock when times got tough. He helped me laugh and smile when times were good, and he was a mighty good father for all of our children. He had a way about him that made the kids respect him and mind what he said, but he never had to be harsh about it. If one of them was out of line, he looked at them a certain way, and they knew to straighten up. It was a gift.

Truth be told, we made a point to never raise our voices in anger at one another or at the children. Plenty of folks do, but that wasn't our way. I'd been through enough of that in my first marriage. Columbus was gentle with me and the kids. It was a peaceful household, and I praise the Lord for it.

I saw a lot of myself in my girls, and I suppose others saw it too. They didn't all love cooking right off, but they were good listeners. I taught them to pour some love into everything they did.

Ive Ville took after Columbus. Columbus was so good about fixing things, building things, taking care of whatever needed to be done—and every step he took,

Ive Ville took a step right behind him. He always wanted to help his daddy.

Little Larry started singing his heart out at an early age. That little boy might've been considered slow in some ways, but the Lord blessed him with an easy love for music.

As they got older, the kids learned to do a little something extra around the house if they wanted to go somewhere or felt like they needed something special. It came to be funny, because we always knew a request was coming if we saw one of them doing any chore that we hadn't asked them to do. Columbus and I had to agree on whatever privilege was asked for, though.

"What'd your daddy say?" I'd ask the little one.

"What'd your mama say?" Columbus would ask, if I wasn't around.

Then, sure enough, we'd usually say: "Whatever your daddy said" or "Whatever your mama said."

We parented together that way and made sure those kids knew we stood on the same side.

Columbus, in particular, made sure the kids never lacked for allowance or the little extras as they got older, no matter how tight the finances were. Shoot, he might've come within an inch of spoiling them, if he'd had the funds to do it. When one of the kids would ask for something, he'd never say, "No, I don't have it." He'd always say, "I'll make a way." And somehow, he did.

It seemed like every Sunday morning before church, Bonnie and Carolyn would say, "Daddy, we need some stockings."

Columbus would say, "Don't y'all know you need stockings on Saturday night?" But he would always walk to the store on Sunday morning and get those girls some stockings.

It happened so often that it tickled us all to no end.

I had my work at Nick's, and Columbus was working those railroads, but we did everything else together. Even some of that was work, I suppose, but it didn't feel like it. We grew and picked vegetables in our garden together—but it wasn't like working the fields when we were younger. It was something we came to enjoy doing, and we were happy to bring fresh vegetables to the table for our children. We'd also go crabbing when the season was right. Those were relaxing times at the edge of the water under a hot Mississippi sun—we'd talk about life and all that we had and all that we still dreamed about. We'd bring back buckets of crabs and cook up a mess of them for the whole family, and everyone would have a big time.

Columbus also got the family a television. It was a little thing with rabbit ears, but it picked up a picture. On Sunday nights at 6:00 pm, we'd all gather around that little TV, adjust the rabbit ears, and watch the Walt Disney special. As the kids grew up, we never missed a Sunday morning at church, and I suppose we never missed a Sunday night Walt Disney special either. That was family time.

Columbus and I walked everywhere—we didn't have a car until 1970—and Lord help us if we went walking up the road without giving our kids a kiss first. They would shout out, "You didn't give us our sugar!" We would turn back around, walk to back to the house, and give them all the kisses they were waiting for.

All of my kids were gifts from God, in my eyes, and Columbus loved all of his children, including those who had a different natural father and those who were disabled—all of his children—with all of the love in his heart. There was a lot of love in that man, and that made me love the man all the more.

I thank the Lord that my children listened, got along, and behaved the way kids ought to behave, aside from a little devilment here and there. Some folks aren't that lucky.

When the children were all old enough to listen and able to follow what I was saying, I took them out to the front yard one day and said, "I want y'all to understand something." I picked up a switch out of the yard and broke it in front of them. I said, "You get one switch, you can break it easily." Then I got a bunch of switches and put them together. I showed them that together they were stronger—that together, they couldn't be broken. I said, "That's what family is all about."

They looked up at me, and I knew right away that my children—all of my children—understood. I'm not sure they even needed the lesson, but I felt it needed saying. Somehow, looking at their sweet faces, I knew that this family of mine would work together and stick together through anything that came our way. I felt it deep down, and that's a mighty wonderful thing to feel.

Something Bigger

As important as family was to us, we always believed community was important too—I think that's something that comes naturally when you live in a small town, especially in the South.

Columbus and I took time with the neighborhood kids, and we enjoyed it. If they needed a little something, we would help them out. Columbus would usually make them work for it, to help them learn the value of a dollar, but he'd pay them whatever little bit they needed. Those kids really came to look up to him.

If a family didn't have food, I'd cook some up for them. I'd even have the mother come by and bring her pots and pans so her kids could think it came from home. I was so happy to do it—shoot, I loved cooking anyway. Circumstances were a little better for us than some of those around us, and I'd spent too many days eating mush as a child to abide a neighbor going hungry if we had food in our cupboard to spare. To me, it would have been a sin to do otherwise. I always wished I could have done more.

As our kids got older, they picked right up on what community meant. They knew they were part of something bigger than our family circle, and they came by caring about others naturally.

I'll tell you something funny, though: Columbus' own love for community did have its limits, because he was mighty picky about who courted our daughters as they got older. The first warning he gave to every young man who ever came courting was that they'd better never raise a hand in violence to one of our girls. He told them if they ever had the urge, they'd better hold back and bring her right back on home to us. Let me tell you, they heeded that warning too.

Columbus had a right to be picky. He was such a good man—*my* good man—and he wanted the same for our girls. So did I, Lord, so did I.

Our roots in the community were running deep— for me, for Columbus, and for the kids. And not just in Foxworth and Marion County, but in the bigger community of southern Mississippi. It was home. It was part of who we were, in blood and spirit—from the people, to the dirt roads, to the hot rolling fields.

I've Got to Get Food on the Grill!

Through the years, I got plenty comfortable working at Nick's, and he got comfortable with me. He was sweet to my kids. His wife, who also worked at the restaurant, was a good woman too. While I was still catching rides to work with Nick, he'd always fly on down the road. If a policeman tried to pull us over, Nick would shout out, "I've got to get food on the grill!" and keep on flying.

Eventually, as Nick got up in age and his wife got sick, I had to take over more and keep the fire. That's when I began to experiment with the barbeque sauce in my own ways. And sure enough, people liked it.

It was a good thing the policemen liked our barbeque too, because we were the cause of other folks speeding on that lane through the years. I heard tell of folks getting pulled over for flying down the road while trying to pick up some of our barbeque before we closed. "I'm tryin' to get to Leatha," they'd say. The police would reply, "You best go on then."

It was a great experience all around. Nick even let my girls help out at the restaurant as they got older. It wasn't our place, exactly, but it felt a lot like family.

After I'd been working for him for about 11 years, Nick had a grill he wanted to sell. So I said, "Mr. Nick, let me have the grill. If I buy this grill, I'm not going to quit working for you. I'll just hang onto it. If I get too old where I can't hold this job, I'll have some way to make a little grocery money."

He was going to sell it anyway, and since I promised him I wouldn't quit, he said, "Well, give me three hundred and one dollars for it, and I'll sell it to you." We had an agreement. I bought that grill, pulled it up to the house, and kept on working for Nick. I made a promise, and I kept it.

That grill sat at our house for three years, and I kept the fire at Nick's. From time to time, my mind would wander, thinking about what I might be able to do with that grill. But my job was making folks happy as they came through the doors of Nick's BBQ, and I loved making folks happy.

It's Never Too Late

*Y*ou never know what'll bring you closer to God. I was always seeking ways to get closer to Him—I always went to church every Sunday, and I always praised the Lord. But I don't think I was filled up with the Holy Spirit until after my sweet little Barbara almost died.

She was already born handicapped and had seizures pretty often, but her toughest battle was yet to come. Her appendix ruptured when she was little, and it was touch-and-go for a long time after that. She was in the hospital for weeks, and the doctors told us that just 5 out of 100 children lived through that sort of thing. I prayed and I cried for my youngest one, but her prospects weren't good.

A friend came by the house, reached in her pocket, and gave me a little piece of paper with an address on it. She said, "Write this preacher." His name was Reverend

Ike. He was on the radio and was well-known in Mississippi in those days. I wrote him and asked him to please
pray for my baby. We started writing back and forth,
and he prayed for little Barbara. Before long, she was
out of that bed, walking again. My baby got better. I
was overjoyed!

I kept on writing back and forth with Reverend Ike,
and he began praying for me—for Leatha. He knew I
wanted a business of my own, so he helped me pray for
that. But what he really wanted to do was to save me.
He would send me Bible verses that had meaning in my
own life, and he would always say, "God ain't in the sky,
God is in you."

I remember the day I felt things turn around—the
moment. I was in the field picking butterbeans, and I
was reading one of Reverend Ike's letters. I felt a change
come over me. It washed over me like a cleansing wave
out there in the Mississippi heat. I looked up, with tears
in my eyes, and I felt the sunlight on my face—and I felt
God. I was saved, once and for all, right there in that
field. God put His hands on me, and I put my full trust in
Him from that day on.

Patience and trust in the Lord is a powerful thing.
Not long after I was touched by God, sweet old Nick
decided to sell his place and retire. All told, I had been

with him for fourteen years. The new owners were nice enough folks, but they wanted to turn it into a different kind of restaurant. We didn't see eye to eye on things, and they didn't need or want my help the same way Nick did.

I had honored my agreement with Nick, and now I had a genuine barbeque grill to use as I pleased. Columbus and I felt like God had delivered that grill to us. We talked and prayed about it some more and realized that the time was finally right to start living out our dream.

It was 1974. I was 51 years old. Columbus was past 60. Some folks thought we were crazy, and plenty more doubted us, but we were going to start our own restaurant.

I'm here to tell you this: if you keep the faith, it's never too late to start doing what you've dreamed about. It's never too late.

Folks Couldn't
Get Enough

Taking a leap and starting our restaurant was slow-going at first. We didn't have a building for it yet, so we set up a grill pit and started selling food right out of the house.

Columbus retired from the railroad. He ran the grill and set his sights on building the restaurant in our field, like we'd talked about through the years. One of Columbus' good friends told him he could tear down an old house of his and use materials from that. That was a blessing. For the rest of the wood, we'd save up from selling food from our home each week, and Columbus would go and buy more boards.

From the get-go, we knew most of our customers would have to be white folks if we were going to have a successful place. Black folks didn't go out for food much in those days, and they didn't tend to have the extra money to spend. Luckily, some of the white folks who were regulars at Nick's got word that I was selling barbeque out of my house, and they started calling.

We didn't seat people at the house—we took orders over the phone. We'd ask for two hours notice, and we'd cook up as much food as they wanted. Then they'd come by and pick it up. After the old Nick's regulars got the word, they started telling their friends. That was our first word of mouth. Word of mouth was what got us started, and we came to realize that word of mouth might be all the advertising we'd ever need.

Truth be told, it was my barbeque sauce, which I'd created in private over the years, that was drawing them in and bringing them back, again and again. I'd fiddled around with that sauce until there wasn't a drop here or a dash there of anything that could make it any better—until it tasted just right to me. That became Leatha's sauce, my own secret recipe, and it was a blessing. There are some things that you just *know* are special. And I just knew, deep down, that my sauce would be a foundation for our future. Folks couldn't get enough of it. They would beg me for the recipe. They would buy extra jars to bring home. There was a genuine love for that sauce—they loved it like some folks love a favorite song.

When we started cooking at the house, I decided to teach my girls the recipe, and I made sure they knew that it was to never leave the family—no matter what. Shoot, I wouldn't even tell Columbus or the boys what that recipe was. The men needed to focus on the grill. The recipe was a secret for me and my daughters ... and maybe, Lord willing, for their daughters some day.

The men learned the secrets of the grill, and those were secrets we decided to keep in the family too. My way of grilling was different than the way I did it with Nick—his way was his way, and my way was my way. I'd figured out a way to keep the meat so tender that it would flat out melt in your mouth. I taught Columbus and Ive Ville that secret ... something for the men in the family to pass down. And it was another big reason folks kept coming back—to taste that sauce poured over tender, falling-off-the-bone pork ribs. Shoot, Columbus got so good at running that grill, and those ribs were so doggone tender, that folks didn't even need teeth to eat them. Older folks could take their dentures out, gum 'em down, and enjoy every morsel.

For two years, we cooked at the house and saved money. Things started slow enough but built up a head of steam like a locomotive chugging down the track. By the time Columbus got that restaurant built, we had a whole bunch of regulars, and we knew that they'd be happy to take a load off, sit for a while, and eat with us instead of just ordering take out. To hear them tell it, they were just as excited as we were ... and after so many years of dreaming, we were ready to open our doors, show them some love, and make them feel right at home, at Leatha's BAR-B-QUE Inn.

They Were More than Customers

Columbus had a gift for building, but the restaurant was never meant to be a fancy place. After all, it was built in a field partly from old lumber and spare supplies. I told folks, "You can drive up, you can look on the outside, and it won't look like it's much. But when you come inside, and when you eat your food, you're going to be satisfied." Through the years, those same folks would tell me that not being fancy was part of the restaurant's "charm," and I came to believe it myself.

It was a real simple place, with tables set around on a wooden floor. Jukeboxes were still popular in those days, but I didn't want one in our place—I didn't want anybody dancing over my customers while they were eating. All I wanted was for Leatha's to be a place where folks could relax and enjoy some barbeque, sweet tea, and good company.

Before we opened up on our first day, I gathered the family around and said, "This restaurant is going to be about love. I love this family. I love to cook. I love people, and that's what makes it. You've got to love people. It ain't all about the food. Love is what's going to make this place special." I knew I didn't have to preach much about that. I was blessed with a family that knew how to show love. It came natural to them.

Myrtis—yes, my little Myrtis—had become a grown woman by the time we opened. She had a husband and a job and, praise the Lord, even children of her own— my first precious grandchildren. Even though she had a full-time job, she came to help out part-time at the restaurant.

Bonnie and Carolyn were nearly grown women themselves, but they were still in school. Bonnie was in college. Carolyn was able to work after school and on Saturdays at first—enough to help me get by.

Columbus and Ive Ville manned the grill. That was the way it was and the way it would always be: the women inside, the men outside on the grill.

We kept the menu simple. Barbeque pork ribs and beef ribs were the main dishes, although we would cook chicken and steaks also. From day one, the hottest seller was the pork ribs, and let me tell you that would never change. I didn't like to waste food, so I didn't keep a lot of vegetables around—I didn't want anything to spoil. I made coleslaw (my own special recipe), fried potatoes, and green salads. I would fix barbeque beans if somebody requested them, and that was it. Folks down south love good old-fashioned barbeque done right, without any frills, and that's what we gave them ... and what we intended to give them for as many years as they'd keep coming.

We had our regular customers right off the bat, but they were more than customers—they were friends. It didn't matter that we were black and they were white; we'd hug them and greet them like they were family, and they'd hug us right back. And it meant something. Mississippi still had problems with black and white folks seeing eye-to-eye, but you wouldn't have known it at our place. It was just a little restaurant in a field, but it was common ground. And there was nothing but love there.

Sometimes people would roll through the door in bunches. Just like my Auntie Emma's restaurant had big crews of regulars from the Bogalusa paper mill and the railroad back in the day, we had big crews of our own come by. Wealthy white businessmen like Bob Kemp and Tommy Wallace became friends and regulars, and they would bring their men in every week to eat. It may not fit with some folks' idea of the south, but friendship and caring doesn't have to be as limited as some believe. Life can surprise you sometimes.

After the restaurant was open for just a few months, we knew we were going to make it. Our regulars were loyal, and new customers were showing up every day. Word of mouth was working its magic. And let me tell you—once business started booming, it kept on booming. The Lord's blessings were spilling over for our family.

We only had thirteen tables, and sometimes people waited two hours just to get inside. People would park on both sides of the lane leading to our restaurant. During the peak hours, they were parked on both sides of the highway leading to the lane, trying to get to Leatha's.

Oil field workers came and tried our barbeque. Once word got out among the oil field workers, it began to spread around Mississippi and beyond.

People were coming in droves from near and far. Some folks were traveling hundreds of miles just to enjoy our food, and they kept coming back.

One night, after closing, Columbus and I stood by the restaurant out in that field under the stars. Everyone had gone home, and it was quiet. We held hands, and we thanked God. We'd been on a long road getting there, but our dream had come true. It was real. We knew what we had, and we knew that our children and our grandchildren would never go hungry or lack for what they really needed in life, because we had created a way to provide that could keep on providing.

As a young girl, I'd worked my fingers to the bone in fields just like that one. As a young boy, Columbus had run for his life through the fields of Mississippi. On that night, we thought about where we'd come from and about how the Lord had led us to a field of our own ... where we stood proud and grateful and fulfilled, and where our lives were bountiful beyond our modest dreams ... and we cried tears of joy.

You've Got to Love It

The fulfillment of our dream was just the beginning of the story of Leatha's Bar-B-Que Inn, naturally. It became a story about family; about my own family and our bigger "family"—the folks who came to eat with us and share their lives with us.

Soon, Bonnie and Carolyn finished school and started working full-time to help me handle the load, and they found the same joy in it that I did. Bonnie loved the front, greeting and meeting the customers, and Carolyn loved the kitchen, just like her Mama.

Carolyn became just as good at making that sauce as me. You couldn't tell a drop of difference. And that girl learned to make a pecan pie that would take your breath away. Whatever cooking talents I had, I passed on to her.

Bonnie never really grew to love cooking, but she sure loved people and she loved working up front—she probably hugged half the folks in Mississippi by the time she was thirty, and she'll hug the other half before she's done.

Those girls poured their love into everything they did, and it gave me so much pride as a mother.

Myrtis poured her love into what she did too. For her, it wasn't all about the restaurant. She'd come in and cook in the evenings, but she was even happier with another job—working at a nursing home, helping old folks. That's what she really came to love. That pleased me greatly too, to tell you the truth. Whatever you do, you've got to love it, and helping others is a beautiful thing.

I had a special bond with my girls; and after my barbeque sauce had become famous around the South, that little secret of ours became a big secret. Companies and wheeler-dealers of all sorts tried to get that recipe out of me. They'd get sneaky about it sometimes, but I was always careful. I never told suppliers who else I was buying from, so no one could ever put together what I put into it—I didn't let the left hand know what the right hand was doing. That secret never slipped out. It stayed with me and my girls, and that's where it will always stay, carrying on to the next generation.

Ive Ville even asked me to tell him that recipe; and as much as I loved my son, I had to smile and hug him and tell him we just couldn't trust it to a man. I said, "Remember Sampson and Delilah? Delilah whispered in Sampson's ear, and he told all of his business. That's why we've got to keep it among us girls."

I never gave Ive Ville that barbeque recipe, but there's nobody I'd trust more than my boy, truth be told. He became a master on the grill, naturally. He learned to cook meat as tender and juicy as Columbus could, and he could fix or build anything, just like Columbus could. And he became a fine, upstanding man in every way.

Yes, I was one proud Mama.

Columbus trained Myrtis's boys on the grill, and that was the beginning of turning Leatha's Bar-B-Que Inn into a family business that could carry on from one generation to the next. To me, that was the sweetest blessing God gave our family—something to carry on.

Bonnie, Carolyn, Ive Ville, Myrtis, and the grandkids helped me and Columbus run the show; but for years, the star of the show, in many folks' eyes, was my boy Larry. When Larry was little, the experts thought he'd never learn to read or write, but he proved the experts wrong. He might have been slow, but he had gifts beyond what the so-called experts or anyone else expected. And Lord Jesus would he sing. We didn't have a jukebox, but we had Larry. And folks would come in partly just to hear him sing on the floor. He serenaded folks every day, and they loved him for it.

Early on, he was affectionately given the nickname "Apple Head," and it stuck. If you want to understand something about the miracles God works, I'm here to tell you that Apple Head became one of the most loved people in all of southern Mississippi.

Larry didn't have a shy bone in his body, and he would ask folks for a dollar to sing for them. Many nights he'd walk out with two or three hundred dollars. People would call in advance to make sure that Larry was singing, because it added so much to their enjoyment.

Larry wound up traveling to different places, singing. He even sang in a chorus at the Super Bowl with Paul McCartney.

He was embraced and adopted by the Southern Mississippi college basketball team. He sang the national anthem sometimes, and he'd sit courtside with the team—they loved him and the fans loved him.

He would tell folks, "I'm famous." His sisters would kid him and say, "Naw, you're just Apple Head."

My little Barbara was watched over by God too, bless her heart. As special as she was, she eventually lost the ability to walk and talk, but we were blessed that The Ellisville State School in Mississippi provided a beautiful and comfortable setting for her to live her life with the constant care she needed, close enough by that we could all spend time with her. You have to see the blessings in life, even if they're hidden under some burden. She was able to get the care she needed, and the love as well.

The good Lord won't give you more than you can handle, and he'll always lift you up in the ways you need it, if you put your trust in him.

I would never claim to be a perfect woman; but if there's a virtue that kept me upright through the years and got me through thick and thin, I suppose it was that one: I always kept my trust in God. Columbus was the same way, and I believe my children learned it too. Never doubt Him for a minute. You'll never cease to be surprised by the blessings He'll bring.

I was blessed with some kind of special family. That much I knew.

We Made It Together

Even though the restaurant became a big success right off, it wasn't always smooth-sailing as the years went on. There was rough water here and there.

In May of 1978, the restaurant burned down. You'd think that setback would have knocked us right out of business, and it did ... but just for two days. The Lord doesn't like idle hands. We used a second home as a temporary location for the restaurant, from May to December. We didn't miss nary a beat. By Christmas, Leatha's Bar-B-Que Inn was re-built, and we rolled right along.

In 1983, there was a flood in Marion County. Well, that closed us down for a couple of days too, but we managed to get things up and running right quickly—and folks were driving and walking through knee-deep water to get some barbeque. Nothing could really knock the restaurant off course. Not fire nor flood nor any other setback. It became a part of people's lives.

A sturdy business can go on and on, I suppose. Unfortunately, it's the people who can't make it forever. The restaurant was still showing strength, but the man who'd built it—twice—was beginning to lose his.

Columbus was mighty proud of me, even though everything we did we did together. He used to smile and tell folks he was married to the most famous woman in Marion County. I don't know if that was true, but I was mighty sure I had the best husband by my side.

Columbus developed diabetes in 1979 and managed it for years. He was on dialysis for a good while too. At one point, he was in the hospital for two months, and I stayed there with him the whole time. I didn't want to leave his side.

In 1989, when he was 79 years old, he lost a leg to it.

The doctors said he would make it, except for losing the leg. But that proud, brave man—the love of my life, the best husband and father to children I could have ever hoped for—told me, "Leatha, I'm not going to put this burden on you. I'm ready to die."

I said, "I might need a little help getting you up, but you won't ever be a burden to me, sweetheart."

Then he said it again: "Leatha. I love you, and I'm not going to put this burden on you."

That was on a Thursday. On Sunday, he was gone. He just made up his mind to let go and let God take him. That took the wind out of me for a while—and some of that wind ain't ever coming back. The life we made, the dreams we saw come true, were only possible because we were together. We made it *together*.

I still thank God every day for the life I had with Columbus.

Everyone deserves to have a love story. That's what I believe. Everyone deserves to find a true love of their own. Brud Jackson was mine. Yes, Lord, Brud Jackson was mine.

The Real Secret Sauce

*L*ove, love, love, love is the most important thing in the world. You've got to love your customer. You've got to love your business. You've got to love your job. You've got to love people—white people, black people, all people.

When folks brought children into Leatha's Bar-B-Que Inn, I saw them as my children, all of them. They all came up together, right there. The customers who came through my doors weren't just customers, they were my friends ... my dear friends.

When you see the same faces every week for thirty years or more, they become like family. That's real. Some of our regulars are famous people, and some are just famous to us, and we love them all the same.

One of our most famous customers, in the world's eyes, is football legend Brett Favre. Some say he's the most famous man in Mississippi, and I don't doubt it. But he's just Brett to us. He's shared a lot of hugs with our family.

We've served other pro football players like the late Steve McNair, and musicians like Wynton Marsalis, and a bunch more famous folks. But when a person asks, "Who's the most famous customer you've had?" We'll say, "You." And we mean it. Nobody is throwing footballs or playing trumpets inside of Leatha's anyway. Folks are there to enjoy the food and the love and the good company. It's as simple as that.

I could go on and on telling stories about our nearest and dearest regulars—our loyal customers and friends—but I'm too worried I'd slip up and leave a dear friend out. They know who they are. They know how special they are to me and to my family. Shoot, they *are* family. They're in my heart.

I suppose I'll tell just one story that's in my heart, without mentioning a name. A young white man who'd come up around our restaurant, and who I'd shared a lot of hugs with through the years, came to visit with me once. I'd known him since he was a child. He had grown up to have a young wife and a child of his own, and he was thinking about committing suicide. I was moved that he turned to me in his time of need, and I felt like

God had directed him to me. I prayed with him on that day, and I called him every night for months after that. That precious young man turned his life around, and he still has a beautiful family. And he has our family too. He knows that he can find love here, whenever he needs it.

At the end of a long road, that's what Leatha's Bar-B-Que Inn is all about. I'm mighty glad folks like the food ... but I'm here to tell you that the real secret sauce doesn't have anything to do with barbeque.

I'm Grateful for the Journey

$\mathcal{I}$'m up there in years now, and I'm going to be joining Brud soon. That's the natural course of things, and I'm at peace with it. I do hope that the dream we built together keeps bringing happiness to folks for many generations to come.

The restaurant moved to Hattiesburg, just a hop and a skip up the road from Foxworth, in 2000. That's where folks can find it these days, and they'll find my family ready to greet them with a warm hug, a warm plate of barbeque, and an ice-cold glass of sweet tea.

I had a hard road early on, but the blessings I've had in life are too many to count. If I could, I'd count them by the people I've shared my love with, from each member of my beautiful family to my many, many wonderful friends.

When I make a friend, I do tend to hang on to them. Remember little Mary Alice, the white girl I was friends with as a child? Well, we were dear friends until she passed in 2010. I suppose when I hug someone, a part of me never lets go. And I've hugged a lot of folks.

I've also suffered some losses, but that's part of life too.

After many years of joy—and singing his sweet heart out—my boy Larry passed away in 2006. It was the saddest thing a mother could experience, but that's when I really understood just how loved he was.

The Southern Mississippi basketball team wore black arm bands to honor him. They closed all of the schools in the area, even the private schools, so that folks could come to his funeral. They bused kids to the funeral, and people stood on the side of the highway to honor Larry. It was on the news as far away as Atlanta.

It's amazing the ways God has touched our lives. And we're still being touched every day, in ways big and small.

Bonnie and Carolyn are still greeting and feeding folks, and Myrtis and Ive Ville are often there too. I've been blessed with wonderful grandkids who'll be carrying on our family tradition as time passes. The good Lord willing, Leatha's Bar-B-Que Inn will live on long past me.

As I get closer to the great hereafter, my mind often drifts back to my days as a young girl, planting seeds in a field under a hot sun, filled with hope about what the future might bring. In my wildest imagination, I couldn't have fathomed just what God had in store for me. I might've imagined success and bounty, in the way a child imagines it, but I never imagined the deep and abiding satisfaction—the pure *joy* I'd find through Brud, my children, my grandchildren, and the people who would walk through our doors and into my life.

I never had to travel far, but I'm standing at the edge of an abundant field now, seeing one last golden sunset, and I'm grateful for the journey.

Yes, Lord, I'm grateful for the journey.

Note from the Publisher

On Saturday, September 14, 2013 Leatha Jackson died shortly after midnight. After 90 years on this earth, she left those who loved her not mourning her passing, but celebrating her incredible life.

Leatha created a destination that was more than just a restaurant; from its first days, there was an ease and a comfort that allowed diners to feel at home the moment they walked through the door. She understood that it may very well be the food that brings them to the table, but it's the warm embrace of family that keeps them coming back for more.

Leatha Jackson's impact on our company extends far beyond the pages of this book. The stories we help to tell, the way we care for readers, the love we share amongst our entire team—these have all been influenced by Leatha's teaching. And although she will never have the opportunity to hold this book—these words—we should all be thankful that her words will continue to hold us.

Leatha Jackson spent most of her life giving of herself for the benefit of others. Now it is our turn to carry on her lessons while she takes her well-deserved rest. So rest on Ms. Leatha ... and thank you for teaching me to "keep the faith" and that in the end, "it's all about love."

—*Indigo River Publishing*

Acknowledgements

$\mathcal{I}$ would like to take this time and opportunity to acknowledge God who is the head of my life, and my family and friends who stood by me every step of the way to help me build this successful business. Had it not been for them and their many hours of sacrifice, Leatha's Bar-B-Que Inn would have never been possible. Therefore, I would like to acknowledge each of them, both management and staff of Leatha's Bar-B-Que Inn. Bonnie Jackson, Myrtis Richardson, Carolyn Stepney, Shareece Stepney, Ive Ville Bickham, Tammy Bickham, Stacy Hardy, Cotrina Morgan, Tisha Jackson, Glenda Dillon, Patrick Jackson, John Brooks, Michael Richardson, Donald Richardson, Greg Richardson, Timothy Jackson, Tommy Jackson, and Brian Jackson.

Made in the USA
Middletown, DE
12 December 2022